Collections for Young Scholars®

READING AND WRITING SKILLS PRACTICE

VOLUME 2

SRA/McGraw-Hill

*A Division of The **McGraw·Hill** Companies*

Copyright © 1998 by SRA/McGraw-Hill.

Printed in the United States of America.

Send all inquiries to:
SRA/McGraw-Hill
250 Old Wilson Bridge Road
Suite 310
Worthington, Ohio 43085

ISBN 0-02-688446-1
  2 3 4 5 6 7 8 9 POH 00 99 98 97

CONTENTS

Skill	Page

Skill	Page

Dialogue

Focus In stories, the dialogue tells us what the characters say.

- The **quotation marks** show the words the character says. Writers put quotation marks at the beginning and at the end of the character's exact words.
- The **speaker tag** tells who said the dialogue.

"I want to be brave," said Toad.

quotation marks   speaker tag

Identify Look in "Dragons and Giants" for examples of dialogue. Write something that Toad said, then write something that Frog said. Discuss the examples with your classmates.

Page: _____

Something that Toad said:

_____

_____

_____

Page: _____

Something that Frog said:

_____

_____

_____

Dialogue (continued)

Practice Read the sentences. In each sentence, underline the words that tell who said the dialogue. Then put quotation marks at the beginning and end of the character's words.

1. I love the Frog and Toad stories, said Beth.

2. They are very funny, Mario agreed. The children talked softly because they were in their classroom.

3. My favorite is *Frog and Toad Are Friends*, said Beth. It always makes me laugh.

4. Mrs. Johnson tapped her pencil. Mario, Beth, do you have something to share with the class? she asked.

5. Well, yes! they said at the same time. We love Frog and Toad!

Apply Write a sentence with dialogue and quotation marks. Be sure to use a speaker tag to tell readers who is speaking.

6. _____

    _____

    _____

    _____

    _____

    _____

Sentence Types

Focus Writers use different kinds of sentences to make stories more interesting.

Sentence Types
- A sentence that **tells** ends with a *period*.
  A snake slid under a rock**.**
- A sentence that **asks** ends with a *question mark*.
  Did you see that snake**?**
- A sentence that **shows strong feeling** ends with an *exclamation point*.
  Don't step on that snake**!**

Identify Look through "Dragons and Giants" for examples of different kinds of sentences. Write one sentence. Does the sentence *tell*, *ask*, or *show strong feeling*? Circle the correct answer. Discuss the sentence with your classmates.

Page: _____

Example sentence: _____

_____

_____

_____

_____

This sentence: tells   asks   shows strong feeling

Sentence Types (continued)

Practice Put the correct mark at the end of each sentence.

1. The frog jumped from the pond_____

2. Can a toad jump_____

3. That toad jumped really high_____

4. How high did that toad jump_____

Apply Use your own words to write different sentence types.

5. Sentence that **tells:**

_____

_____

_____

_____

6. Sentence that **asks:**

_____

_____

_____

_____

7. Sentence that **shows strong feeling:**

_____

_____

_____

_____

Verbs

Focus All complete sentences need a verb.

> A **verb** names an action or tells what someone or something is, was, or will be.
>
>   Kevin **rides** a bike.
>   The bike **is** blue.

Practice Look through a story you have read. Find and list the verbs in the sentences.

1. _____

2. _____

3. _____

4. _____

5. _____

6. _____

Underline the verb in each sentence.

7. Jerry hit the baseball.

8. The sea was calm.

9. Serena pours a glass of milk.

10. The kittens are adorable.

11. She fed her dog.

12. A whale splashed in the sea.

13. Red cars race around the track.

14. We gave flowers to Aunt Betty.

Verbs (continued)

Use a verb from the box to complete each sentence.

15. Alfonso _____ seven years old.

16. Grace _____ a bucket with water.

17. The wind _____ Grandpa's hat into the lake.

18. A cheetah _____ very fast.

19. My sister _____ to the park yesterday.

runs	is	went	filled	blew

Apply Use each verb in a sentence of your own.

20. laugh _____

_____

_____

21. saw _____

_____

_____

22. spill _____

_____

_____

Capitalization

Focus Good writers know when to use capital letters.

- The first word in a sentence always begins with a **capital letter.**
      Ocean water is salty.

- The word *I* is always a capital letter.
      Yesterday **I** went swimming.

- Names of people and places begin with a capital letter.
      Mr. Jim Johnson, Rochester, New York

- Days of the week and months of the year begin with a capital letter.
      Monday, August 12

Practice Look in a story you have read. Find and write a sentence that shows each correct use of a capital letter.

Sentence that names a person or a place:

1. _____

   _____

   _____

Sentence that names a day of the week or a month:

2. _____

   _____

   _____

Capitalization (continued)

Each of the following sentences has two capitalization errors.
Rewrite each sentence using correct capitalization.

3. i named my puppy ralphie.

_____

4. Our school is on main street.

_____

5. thanksgiving is always in november.

_____

6. i played outside on saturday.

_____

Apply Write a sentence to answer each question. Use capital letters correctly.

7. What is your name?

_____

8. When were you born?

_____

9. What is the name of your school?

_____

10. What is your teacher's name?

_____

Name _____ Date _____

Characterization

Focus The more you know about characters in stories, the more you can understand and enjoy the stories.

> Writers let readers know about a character by describing the way the character **looks, talks,** and **acts.**

Identify Look through *The Hole in the Dike* for examples of how the author tells readers about a character. Write a sentence that tells something about the character, then write the name of the character. Discuss with your classmates what the sentence tells about the character.

Page: _____

Sentence that tells about the character: _____

_____

_____

_____

_____

Character's name: _____

Characterization (continued)

Practice Read the story. Then draw a line to connect the character's name with the correct description.

     Wilkin Wooley was afraid. It was his first day in a new school. Mr. Thurmond, the principal, was kind and helpful. He walked Wilkin to the second-grade classroom.

     When Mr. Thurmond introduced Wilkin to the class, Brad, a boy in the back of the room, giggled. "Wilkin Wooley," he whispered loudly. "What a silly name! It's a name for a sheep. Baa." No one in the class laughed.

     At lunch, another boy asked Wilkin to sit at the table with him. "Hi, I'm Al," he said. "And I think your name is neat." Soon three more of Wilkin's classmates sat down at the table. They were all friendly.

1. Wilkin
    is kind and helpful

2. Brad
    asks Wilkin to sit with him at lunch

3. Mr. Thurmond
    teases Wilkin about his name

4. Al
    is afraid because it is his first day in a new school

Apply Write a sentence that shows how Wilkin might have acted after he found new friends at school.

5. _____

_____

_____

_____

Reading and Writing Skills Practice

Parts of a Sentence

Focus   A sentence must have a subject and a predicate.

- The **subject** tells who or what.
- The **predicate** tells what the subject does or what happened. A predicate always has a verb.

The dog barked.

subject   predicate

Practice   Read each sentence. Draw a line under the subject and circle the predicate.

1. James walked to the park.

2. He saw a pond.

3. A fish swam in the water.

4. The water was cold.

5. Squirrels watched from a tree.

6. Thunder roared.

7. Rain fell on James.

8. He ran home.

9. Lions chase the zebras.

10. Nicky rides a brown horse.

Parts of a Sentence (continued)

Write a subject to complete each sentence.

11. The _____ rang.

12. _____ got out of bed.

13. _____ looked outside.

14. _____ was falling!

15. _____ wore a coat to school.

Write a verb to complete the predicate in each sentence.

16. Gary _____ a puppy.

17. He _____ it home.

18. The puppy _____ some water.

19. It _____ with Gary's sister.

20. They both _____ the puppy.

21. Big fish _____ in the sea.

Apply Write a sentence of your own. Underline the subject
and circle the verb.

22. _____

_____

_____

_____

Adjectives

Focus Good writers use adjectives to make their writing more interesting.

> An **adjective** describes a noun or a pronoun.
> Carlos bakes **delicious** cookies.
> Fran has a **little** kitten.
> Amy ate the **last** apple.

Practice Circle the adjective in each sentence.

1. Manuel needed a new jacket.

2. He went to the big store.

3. He liked a red jacket.

4. It had a broken zipper.

Write an adjective to complete each sentence.

5. Chelsea wanted to bake _____ bread.

6. She needed some _____ milk.

7. She poured the milk into a _____ bowl.

8. She put the dough in a _____ pan.

9. The bread baked in a _____ oven.

10. _____ bread tastes good with milk.

Adjectives (continued)

Apply Use each adjective in a sentence.

11. happy _____

_____

_____

12. wet _____

_____

_____

13. yellow _____

_____

_____

14. first _____

_____

_____

15. big _____

_____

_____

Reading and Writing Skills Practice

Compound Words

Focus   Using compound words can make your writing more interesting.

> A **compound word** is one word made of two words joined together.
>
> with + out = without
> air + plane = airplane
> birth + day = birthday

Practice   Circle each compound word.

1.   rainbow   haircut   cookie

train   homesick   maybe

Use the picture clues to make compound words. Write the compound word.

 +

2. _____

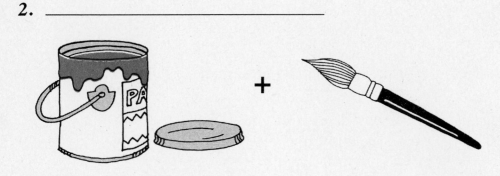

3. _____

Compound Words (continued)

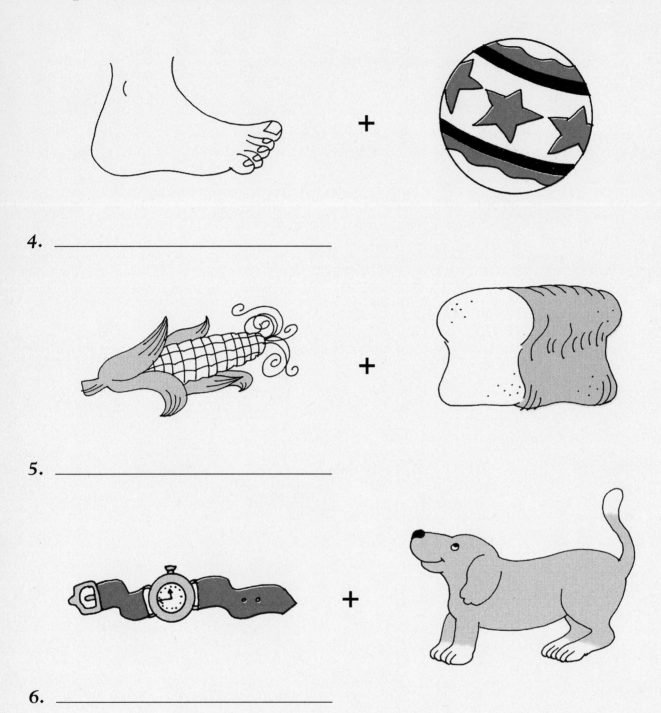

4. _____

5. _____

6. _____

Apply Write a sentence using one of the compound words
you wrote.

7. _____

_____

_____

Reading and Writing Skills Practice

Name _____ Date _____

Giving Opinions

Focus In stories, opinions tell us what characters think.

Writers sometimes show a character **giving opinions** of other characters and events in the story to help readers understand the characters and enjoy the story more.

I think baseball is the best sport.

Identify Look in *Molly the Brave and Me* for examples of opinions that tell how a character feels or thinks. Write a sentence that tells what Beth thinks about Molly. Then write a sentence that tells what Molly thinks about Beth. Discuss the examples with your classmates.

Page: _____

Sentence that tells what Beth thinks about Molly:

_____

_____

_____

Page: _____

Sentence that tells what Molly thinks about Beth:

_____

_____

_____

Giving Opinions (continued)

Practice and Apply Read the story, then write the answers to
the questions.

Deborah looked in the mirror. She took a deep breath.
Today she was going to give a speech at school.

"I am so nervous. I don't like making speeches,"
Deborah said to her mother.

Later, Mr. Perez announced, "Our next speaker is
Deborah Manso."

Deborah walked to the stage. She began her speech.
She thought her voice was too loud. She thought her knees
were shaking. But she remembered her whole speech.

"Very good job, Deborah," Mr. Perez said.

"I'm so proud of you!" said her mother.

"Making speeches is fun," said Deborah.

1. What did Mr. Perez think of Deborah's speech?

   _____

   _____

2. How did Deborah's mother feel about her?

   _____

   _____

3. How did Deborah feel about speeches before she made her
   speech?

   _____

   _____

4. How did Deborah feel about speeches after she made her speech?

   _____

   _____

Reading and Writing Skills Practice

Dialogue

Focus In stories, the dialogue tells readers exactly what the characters say.

> - The **quotation marks** show the exact words the character says.
> - The **speaker tag** tells who said the dialogue.
>   "This was once a church," said Mike.

Identify Look in *Molly the Brave and Me* for examples of dialogue. Write a sentence of dialogue that Beth says, then write a sentence of dialogue that Molly says. Discuss the examples with your classmates.

Page: _____

Sentence of dialogue that Beth says: _____

_____

_____

_____

Sentence of dialogue that Molly says: _____

_____

_____

_____

_____

Dialogue (continued)

Practice Read the passage. Put quotation marks at the beginning and end of each line of dialogue. Underline the words that tell who is speaking.

Welcome to the Nature Club hike, said the park ranger. Today's hike is to the top of Hillside Point. Are there any questions?

Louise called out, How far is it to the top?

It is almost one mile, answered the ranger. It will take about an hour to reach the top.

Maybe we will be able to see the town from the top, wondered Louise.

Apply Pretend you are Molly in the story *Molly the Brave and Me*. Write a sentence of dialogue that Molly might say to Beth. Be sure to write a speaker tag.

_____

_____

_____

_____

_____

Contractions

Focus Knowing how to make and use contractions can help you be a better writer.

- A **contraction** is one word made of two words put together. One or more letters are left out.
- An **apostrophe (')** takes the place of the missing letters.
    I am happy to see you.
    I'm happy to see you. (I + am = I'm)

Practice Draw a line to match each pair of words to the correct contraction.

1. we are		it's
2. you are		I've
3. I have		you're
4. he is		he's
5. she will		I'll
6. it is		she'll
7. I will		we're

Read each sentence and write the words that make up each contraction.

8. I know where she's going. _____

9. He'll be at work all day. _____

Contractions (continued)

Rewrite each sentence. Write a contraction in place of the underlined words.

10. <u>I have</u> read this book three times.

_____

_____

11. Our teacher said <u>we are</u> going to the museum.

_____

_____

12. <u>You are</u> a good friend.

_____

_____

13. The doctor said <u>I will</u> feel better tomorrow.

_____

_____

Apply   Write a sentence of your own using a contraction.

14. _____

_____

_____

Writing Paragraphs

Sally Ride, Astronaut: An American First

Focus All the sentences in a paragraph tell about one main idea.

- A **paragraph** is a group of sentences that all go together.
- The **main idea** tells what the paragraph is about.

Identify Choose two paragraphs from *Sally Ride, Astronaut: An American First*. Read each paragraph and write the main idea of the paragraph.

Page: _____   Paragraph: _____

The main idea is: _____

_____

_____

_____

Page: _____   Paragraph: _____

The main idea is: _____

_____

_____

_____

Writing Paragraphs (continued)

Practice Read the paragraph. Then draw a line under the most important sentence in the paragraph. It is the main idea.

   Astronauts must wear a special suit in space. The space suit covers their whole body. A face mask lets them see. Their space suit must keep them warm. It must have air for the astronaut to breathe. Outside the space craft, astronauts wear a backpack attached to the space suit. It is jet-powered to help the astronaut move around in space.

Apply What other information does the paragraph give? Use your own words to tell one detail about the special suits that astronauts wear.

_____

_____

_____

_____

_____

_____

Reading and Writing Skills Practice

Topic Sentences

Focus A good topic sentence helps readers know what a paragraph is about.

A **topic sentence**
- gives the **main idea** of the paragraph. The other sentences in a paragraph give details or information about the main idea.
- is often the **first sentence** of a paragraph. Placing the topic sentence first helps readers know what the paragraph is about.

Practice Read each paragraph. Underline the topic sentence in each one.

1. Carly collects stamps. She likes U.S. stamps and stamps from other countries. When a letter comes to her house, she always checks the stamp. She is happy when she finds a new stamp to keep.

2. Navy blue is Matt's favorite color. He has navy blue walls in his bedroom. His bedspread has navy blue stripes. He has navy blue tennis shoes. Even his toothbrush is navy blue.

3. Nancy likes music very much. She plays the trombone and the recorder. On Saturday, she goes to dance class. She wants to learn to play the piano.

Topic Sentences (continued)

Read the paragraph below. Notice that it is missing a topic sentence. Choose the correct topic sentence from the box and write it on the lines below.

4. _____

_____

_____

In one day, a young grasshopper eats twice its own weight. If you weighed 60 pounds, you would have to eat 120 pounds of food to eat as much as a young grasshopper eats.

> Grasshoppers don't get much sleep.
> A grasshopper has a big appetite.
> Spiders eat ants.
> You could be a grasshopper.

Apply Write one topic sentence of your own for the paragraph above. Make sure your sentence tells about the main idea of the paragraph.

5. _____

_____

_____

_____

Name _____ Date _____

Point of View

Focus Point of view is the position or viewpoint from which a storyteller tells a story. A story may be told from the first-person point of view or the third-person point of view.

When a story is told from the **first-person point of view**
- the storyteller is a character in the story
- the words *I* and *we* are used

    I ran to the barn to check the cows.

When a story is told from the **third-person point of view**
- the storyteller is not a character in the story
- the words *she*, *he*, and *they* are used

  There was a child lost in the woods, and he was afraid.

Identify Look in "The Three Wishes" for clue words that let you know who is telling the story. Write the words and tell whether the story is told from the first-person point of view or the third-person point of view. Discuss with your classmates how you know who is telling the story.

Page: _____   Clue words: _____

From what point of view is the story told? _____

_____

_____

_____

Point of View (continued)

Practice   Read each sentence. Fill in the circle to tell if the sentence is written from the first-person point of view or the third-person point of view. Underline the word or words in each sentence that helps you know the point of view.

1. Early one morning, a magic fairy appeared in my mirror.
  ○ first-person point of view
  ○ third-person point of view

2. She looked at her long hair in the mirror.
  ○ first-person point of view
  ○ third-person point of view

3. Tim and I held a jumping contest for frogs and grasshoppers.
  ○ first-person point of view
  ○ third-person point of view

Apply   Write one sentence from the third-person point of view.

4. _____

_____

_____

_____

Write one sentence from the first-person point of view.

5. _____

_____

_____

_____

End Punctuation

Focus Every sentence has a punctuation mark at the end. The kind of mark depends on the kind of sentence.

- A sentence that tells something ends with a **period.**
    Cory gave me a book about whales**.**
- A sentence that asks a question ends with a **question mark.**
    Does it have many pictures**?**
- A sentence that shows strong feeling ends with an **exclamation point.**
    Yes, it's a terrific book**!**

Practice Read each sentence and put the correct punctuation mark at the end. Fill in the circle to show if the sentence tells something, asks a question, or shows strong feeling.

1. How is the weather today_____
    ○ tells   ○ asks   ○ shows strong feeling

2. I will look out the window_____
    ○ tells   ○ asks   ○ shows strong feeling

3. It's pouring_____
    ○ tells   ○ asks   ○ shows strong feeling

4. Pam saw the nurses_____
    ○ tells   ○ asks   ○ shows strong feeling

5. If we go, will we see the tigers_____
    ○ tells   ○ asks   ○ shows strong feeling

End Punctuation (continued)

Read each sentence and put the correct punctuation mark at the end.

6. A ladybug is a helpful insect_____

7. Did you know it eats aphids_____

8. What are aphids_____

9. Aphids are tiny insects that can kill plants_____

10. Wow, one ladybug eats 600 aphids in its life_____

11. Aphids are white, and ladybugs are red_____

12. Do ladybugs fly_____

Apply Follow the directions to write new sentences.

13. Write a sentence that ends with a period.

_____

_____

14. Write a sentence that ends with a question mark.

_____

_____

15. Write a sentence that ends with an exclamation point.

_____

_____

Name _____ Date _____

Descriptive Words   "The Goose That Laid the Golden Eggs"

Focus Writers use descriptive words to help readers picture things that happen in the story.

- **Descriptive words** such as *red*, *first*, and *some* are called adjectives.
- **Adjectives** answer the questions *what kind? which one?* or *how many?*

Adjective	Answers the question
red	what kind?
first	which one?
some	how many?

Identify Look in "The Goose That Laid the Golden Eggs" for examples of descriptive words. Write examples of descriptive words. Then fill in the circle to tell which question the descriptive word answers. Discuss the examples with your classmates.

Page: _____

Descriptive word _____
   ○ what kind?   ○ which one?   ○ how many?

Descriptive word _____
   ○ what kind?   ○ which one?   ○ how many?

Descriptive word _____
   ○ what kind?   ○ which one?   ○ how many?

Descriptive word _____
   ○ what kind?   ○ which one?   ○ how many?

Descriptive Words (continued)

Practice and Apply   Write a descriptive word in each blank to complete the passage. Use adjectives from the box or use your own words.

Grace was excited. Today, for the _____

time, she is going to walk to the store. Her

_____ brother Gordon is coming, too.

The store is _____ blocks from home.

Grace puts _____ money in her pocket.

Mother wants them to buy some _____

juice. Grace wants to buy a _____

muffin. She will surprise Gordon with a

_____ bar. They can eat their snacks on

the _____ walk home.

big	first	three	granola
some	blueberry	short	fresh

Reading and Writing Skills Practice

Point of View

Focus Point of view is the position or viewpoint from which a storyteller tells a story. A story is told from a first-person point of view or a third-person point of view.

First-Person Point of View
- A character in the story is telling the story. The storyteller tells about his or her own thoughts or feelings.
- The storyteller uses the words *I*, *me*, *we*, *our*, and *us*.

Third-Person Point of View
- The storyteller is not a character in the story. The storyteller tells about things that happen to other people in the story.
- The storyteller uses the words *he*, *she*, *him*, *her*, *they*, *their*, *then*, and *them*.

Identify Look through a story you have read. Who is telling the story? Is it a character in the story or someone outside the story? Is the story told from the first-person point of view or third-person point of view?

Story: _____

1. Who is telling the story? _____

2. Is the storyteller in the story? _____

3. What is the storyteller's point of view? _____

Point of View (continued)

Practice Read each story part. Write the point of view the storyteller is using. Is it the first-person point of view or third-person point of view?

4. The scouts set up their tent. They had to gather wood for a campfire. That night they toasted marshmallows and sang songs.

   What is the point of view? _____

5. Suddenly the lights went out. Dad asked me to get the flashlight. I was glad it had new batteries.

   What is the point of view? _____

6. The bus ride took a long time. We thought we'd never get there. I was glad that Steve and Carla asked me to sit with them.

   What is the point of view? _____

7. Jamal peeked around the corner. The sidewalk was empty. Now he could practice skating. No one would laugh if he fell.

   What is the point of view? _____

Apply Write one sentence from the first-person point of view.

8. _____

   _____

   _____

Name _____ Date _____

Punctuating Dialogue

Tool Card 62

Focus In stories, what the characters say to each other is called dialogue. The exact words the characters say are quotations.

Quotation marks (" ") begin and end a character's exact words in a story.

- The first word in a quotation always begins with a **capital letter.**
- The **end punctuation** goes inside the quotation mark.
- A **comma** separates the quotation from the rest of the sentence.

Ted said, "Tell me where you live."

or

"Tell me where you live," said Ted.

or

"Where do you live?" asked Ted.

Practice Put quotation marks around the dialogue in each sentence.

1. Do you like pasta? asked Barney.

2. Shirelle said, I like almost everything.

3. Mom called, Dinner is ready.

4. Let's eat! Barney said.

5. Please pass the cheese, said Shirelle.

6. Barney asked, Is there any more sauce?

Punctuating Dialogue (continued)

Rewrite each sentence using dialogue. Use capital letters,
quotation marks, and commas where needed.

7. Billy said we should make a class newspaper.

_____

_____

8. Jonah said that is a good idea.

_____

_____

9. Debbie asked can I write a story?

_____

_____

Apply Write a sentence with dialogue. Use punctuation marks
and capital letters correctly.

10. _____

_____

_____

Sentence Types

Focus Writers use different kinds of sentences to make stories more interesting.

Sentence Types
- A sentence that **tells** something ends with a *period*.
  The elephant danced at the circus.
- A sentence that **asks** a question ends with a *question mark*.
  Will you go to the circus with me?
- A sentence that **shows strong feeling** ends with an *exclamation point*.
  Yes, I will!

Identify Look in *The Empty Pot* for examples of different kinds of sentences. Write one example of each sentence type.

Page: _____

Sentence that tells: _____

_____

Page: _____

Sentence that asks: _____

_____

Page: _____

Sentence that shows strong feeling: _____

_____

Sentence Types (continued)

Practice and Apply Look at the picture. Follow the directions to write three types of sentences that go with the picture.

1. Write a sentence that *tells* to go with the picture.

_____

_____

_____

2. Write a sentence that *asks a question* to go with the picture.

_____

_____

_____

3. Write a sentence that *shows strong feeling* to go with the picture.

_____

_____

_____

Reading and Writing Skills Practice

Setting

Focus Writers describe the setting to give readers a better picture of the story.

> The **setting** of a story is the time and place in which a story happens.

Identify Look in *The Empty Pot* for examples that describe the setting. Write two sentences that show how the author describes when and where the story takes place. Discuss the examples with your classmates.

Page: _____

Sentence that tells when the story takes place:

_____

_____

_____

_____

Page: _____

Sentence that tells where the story takes place:

_____

_____

_____

_____

Setting (continued)

Read the story and answer the questions. Then describe the setting in your own words.

Last summer, James and his scout troop visited a tropical forest. They went on a three-mile hike. The forest was thick with trees. It was dark, even in the morning. Not one ray of sun could get through the trees. Sometimes, James couldn't see the trail. He followed the forest ranger carefully. James became very interested in the forest around him. He decided to find out how to become a forest ranger.

1. When did this story take place?

_____

_____

2. Where did this story take place?

_____

_____

3. Describe the setting in your own words.

_____

_____

_____

Name _____ Date _____

Plot

Focus In a story, the plot is made up of the things that happen in the story.

> The **plot** of a story
> - usually begins by introducing the **main characters,** the **setting,** and the **problem** that must be solved.
> - usually ends with a **climax** or high point of the story and a **solution** to the problem.

Identify Look in *Cinderella* for the main characters, the setting, and the problem in the story. Then list the main characters, setting, and problem below.

Main characters:

_____

_____

_____

_____

Setting:

_____

_____

Problem:

_____

_____

Plot (continued)

Practice and Apply Choose another fairy tale you know. Write the answers to the questions about the plot in your own words.

Story title: _____

Main characters: _____

1. **Setting:** Where and when does the story take place?

   _____

   _____

2. **Problem:** What is the problem in the story?

   _____

   _____

   _____

3. **Main event:** What is the climax or high point?

   _____

   _____

   _____

4. **End of problem:** How is the problem solved?

   _____

   _____

   _____

Reading and Writing Skills Practice

Name _____ Date _____

Writing Paragraphs

Cinderella

Focus A paragraph is a group of sentences that tell about the same topic or subject.

- In a **paragraph,** usually one sentence tells the **main idea**—what the whole paragraph is about.
- The sentence that gives the main idea of the whole paragraph is called the **topic sentence.**

Identify Choose two paragraphs from *Cinderella* and write the main idea of each paragraph. You may choose one sentence in the paragraph or you may use your own words.

Page: _____   Paragraph: _____

The main idea is: _____

_____

_____

_____

Page: _____   Paragraph: _____

The main idea is: _____

_____

_____

_____

Writing Paragraphs (continued)

Practice Read the paragraph. Then write the main idea.

Once upon a time, a little girl lived alone in the forest.
She had lived in the forest for so long, she thought she must
have been born there. The birds and the squirrels were her
family. They shared their food with her. They built her a
bed padded with twigs and feathers and leaves. It was as soft
as any bed could be.

1. The main idea of the paragraph is: _____

_____

_____

Apply Write a paragraph. Use the sentence below as the main
idea. Add other sentences that tell about the main idea to
make an interesting paragraph.

2. One spring day, all the birds in the trees began to sing the

same song. _____

_____

_____

_____

Reading and Writing Skills Practice

Persuasive Writing

Focus Sometimes writers want to make their readers think, feel, or act in a certain way. They want to persuade their readers.

> There are two ways to **persuade** readers to agree with the idea you are writing about.
> - Tell **why** the idea is a good one.
> - Tell **your own feelings and thoughts** about the idea.

Practice Think of an idea that you want your readers to agree with. Make notes about why it is a good idea and how you feel about the idea.

1. Idea: _____

_____

_____

2. Why this is a good idea: _____

_____

_____

3. My own feelings about this idea: _____

_____

_____

Persuasive Writing (continued)

Apply Use the idea you wrote on page 51 and write a
paragraph in which you try to persuade your readers to agree
with the idea. Decide whether to give good reasons or to tell
your own feelings.

4. _____

_____

_____

_____

_____

_____

_____

_____

_____

_____

_____

_____

Reading and Writing Skills Practice

Capitalization

Focus Good writers know when to use capital letters.

- The first word in a sentence always begins with a **capital letter.**
    The sky is blue.
- The word *I* is always a capital letter.
    This is the place where **I** fell.
- Names of people and places begin with a capital letter.
    Mrs. Wilma Trader, Ridge Hill, Ohio
- Days of the week and months of the year begin with a capital letter.
    Sunday, September 1

Practice Look through a story you have read. Find and write a sentence that shows each correct use of a capital letter.

Sentence beginning with a capital letter:

1. _____

   _____

Sentence with the word *I*:

2. _____

   _____

Sentence that names a person or a place:

3. _____

   _____

Reading and Writing Skills Practice

Capitalization (continued)

Each of the following sentences has three capitalization errors.
Rewrite each sentence using the correct capitalization.

4. Janis was born in new york city.

_____

5. her father moved from england in january.

_____

6. she goes to the lincoln school.

_____

7. the bridge was closed on tuesday, march 30.

_____

Apply Write a sentence to answer each question. Use capital
letters correctly.

8. What days of the week do you go to school?

_____

9. What is the name of a famous movie star?

_____

Name _____ Date _____

Problems and Solutions

Focus In many stories, the characters have a problem to solve. Sometimes more than one problem is solved.

- **Problems** are difficult things that happen to a character or characters in a story.
- **Solutions** are ways the character deals with the problem.

Identify In "Amadou's Story" there is one big problem to solve and some little ones. Read the chart to see how problem 1 is solved. Then look in "Amadou's Story" for the solution to problem 2 in the chart. Write the solution.

Problem	Solution
1. When there is no rain to grow grain, the people of N'Dimb are hungry.	They learn to store extra grain, so there will be food when there is no rain.
2. The people of N'Dimb had no place to keep extra grain.	_____ _____ _____ _____ _____ _____ _____

Problems and Solutions (continued)

Practice and Apply Read the story and find the problem and the solution.

Every day, Michael liked to walk in the park near his home. He liked to listen to the birds. He liked the fresh air.

But there was one thing Michael didn't like about the park. Sometimes, the park was dirty. The trash cans were full. Pieces of trash blew on the grass. People did not clean up after their dogs.

One day in class, Mrs. Zheng said they would have a picnic on Friday in the park. Michael raised his hand and told Mrs. Zheng about the dirty park.

"I have an idea," said Antonia. "Let's meet after school on Thursday and clean up the park."

On Thursday, Mrs. Zheng and the whole class met at the park. They all worked together to clean up the park. They put up a sign that said *Please Clean Up After Your Dog.* They made the park a beautiful place.

Use your own words to tell the problem. _____

_____

_____

_____

_____

Use your own words to tell how the problem was solved.

_____

_____

_____

_____

Expressing Characters' Thoughts and Feelings

Focus Reading about the thoughts and feelings of characters helps us understand the characters better.

> Writers often tell the **thoughts and feelings** of the characters in stories by showing what the characters say and do.

Identify Look through "Amadou's Story" for the sentence that tells how Amadou feels about storytellers. Discuss with your classmates what the example tells you about the character's feelings.

Page: _____

Sentence that tells how Amadou feels about storytellers:

_____

_____

_____

_____

_____

_____

Expressing Characters' Thoughts and Feelings
(continued)

Practice and Apply Look at each picture. Use your own words
to write a sentence that tells the thoughts and feelings of the
character in each picture.

1. _____

_____

_____

2. _____

_____

_____

3. _____

_____

_____

Pronouns

Focus Pronouns are words that take the place of nouns. Using the right pronoun makes your meaning clear.

- A **singular (one) pronoun** takes the place of a singular noun.

    Joey played ball. He had a good time.
- **Plural (more than one) pronouns** take the place of plural nouns.

    Joey and Celia played ball. They had fun.

Practice Underline the pronoun in each sentence. Circle the noun or nouns that each pronoun replaces.

1. Betsy lost her kitten.

2. Mark placed his book on the table.

3. Mary and Katie live in that building. They are sisters.

4. This window is stuck. Please close it.

5. Kyle is ready. When will Uncle Bill meet him?

6. Did Max bake the cake? It is good!

7. The books are about animals. They have lots of pictures.

8. Will Mike and Liz drive when they take a trip?

Pronouns (continued)

Read each numbered sentence. Place an X next to the sentence below it that uses the correct pronoun to replace the underlined word.

9. The <u>squirrels</u> watched the dog.

    _____ They watched the dog.

    _____ It watched the dog.

10. The <u>sunset</u> was beautiful.

    _____ It was beautiful.

    _____ She was beautiful.

Apply Read each sentence. Draw a line through each pronoun that does not agree with the word or words in dark letters it replaces. Write the correct pronoun above the one you crossed out.

11. **Mrs. Rabbit** gathered carrots. He fed the carrots to the bunnies.

12. **Ralph and Tim** have a pet mouse. He took the mouse to school.

13. **Mr. Angelo** wants to go to the party. It has a present for Beth.

14. **Scott and I** went hiking. She spent the day on a trail.

Adjectives

Focus Writers use adjectives to make their writing more interesting.

- **Descriptive words** such as *strong*, *oldest*, and *three* are called **adjectives.**
- Adjectives answer the questions *what kind? which one?* or *how many?*

Identify Look in "The Golden Goose" for adjectives.

Page: _____

Write three adjectives that describe the first two sons.

_____

_____

_____

Page: _____

Write one adjective that describes the third son.

_____

Page: _____

Write two adjectives that describe the old man.

_____

_____

Adjectives (continued)

Practice Write a descriptive word in each blank to complete
the story. Use adjectives from the box or use your own words.

On her way home from school, Judy saw a

_____ box. She heard a

_____ sound coming from the box. Judy

was a _____ girl, so she peeked in the

box. To her surprise, she saw _____

kittens! Judy reached in to feel their

_____ fur. She didn't even notice the

_____ boy standing near the box.

"Do you know anyone who can give a kitten a

_____ home?" asked the boy.

brown	tiny	curious	four
baby	soft	teenage	good

Apply Write a sentence using an adjective.

_____

_____

_____

Giving Explanations

Focus Writers give explanations to make their ideas clearer to readers.

> **Explanations** tell how something is done, give the reasons why something is the way it is, or give information about what something means.

Identify Look in *Fossils Tell of Long Ago* for an example of an explanation of how something is done. Tell about the example you choose.

Page: _____

What is being explained? _____

_____

_____

_____

_____

_____

_____

Giving Explanations (continued)

Practice Look in *Fossils Tell of Long Ago* for the explanation of how a dinosaur track becomes a fossil. Write the steps.

_____

_____

_____

_____

_____

Apply Think about something you do or know well. Explain how it is done.

_____

_____

_____

_____

_____

Reading and Writing Skills Practice

Name _____   Date _____

Giving Definitions

Focus In stories, the more you know about what the words mean, the more likely you are to understand and enjoy the stories.

- A **definition** gives the *meaning* of a word.
- In stories, writers **give definitions** of words or phrases that may be hard for readers to understand.

Identify Look through *Fossils Tell of Long Ago* for examples in which the author gives a definition of a word or a phrase. Write two examples. Discuss the examples with your classmates.

Page: _____

Word or phrase that is defined: _____

Definition that is given: _____

_____

_____

Page: _____

Word or phrase that is defined: _____

Definition that is given: _____

_____

_____

Giving Definitions (continued)

Practice Look in *Fossils Tell of Long Ago* and find the definitions the author gives for the two words below. Write the definition for each word.

1. amber _____

_____

_____

2. extinct _____

_____

_____

Apply Write a definition for two words whose meanings you know.

3. Word: _____

Definition: _____

_____

4. Word: _____

Definition: _____

_____

Reading and Writing Skills Practice

Parts of Speech

Focus Language is made up of different kinds of words called parts of speech.

- A **noun** names a person, place, or thing.
    John rides the bus.

- A **pronoun** takes the place of a noun.
    He rides the bus.

- A **verb** names an action or tells what someone or something is, was, or will be.
    John rides the bus.
    John is a student.

- An **adjective** describes a noun or pronoun.
    He rides a yellow bus.

- An **adverb** describes a verb. It may answer the questions *how? how often? when?* or *where?*
    John often rides the bus.

Practice Underline the word in each sentence that is the part of speech listed on the left.

1. adverb   A snail moves slowly across the sidewalk.

2. noun   The grasshopper jumped away.

3. adjective   An elephant has a long trunk.

4. verb   We painted the old gray barn.

5. pronoun   Ellen wore her hat.

Parts of Speech (continued)

Read the paragraph. Find at least one word from the paragraph for each part of speech. Write each word in the correct place in the chart.

Eve made the costumes for the school play. She worked quickly. The costumes looked beautiful.

noun	pronoun	verb	adjective	adverb

Apply Complete each sentence. Write a word that is the part of speech listed to the left.

6. adjective   It was a very _____ day.

7. verb   The scouts decided to _____ to the park.

8. adverb   They hiked _____ up the hill.

9. noun   At the top, they saw a _____.

10. pronoun   _____ was beautiful.

11. adjective   My cat has _____ eyes.

12. verb   Insects _____ on the plants.

Reading and Writing Skills Practice

Verbs

Focus Past-tense verbs show action that has already happened.

- Many **past-tense verbs** end in *-ed*.

    walked

- For most one-syllable verbs that have one short vowel and one final consonant, **double the final consonant and add *-ed*.**

    tapped

- If the verb ends with a consonant followed by *y*, **change the *y* to *i* and add *-ed*.**

    cried

- Some verbs have special forms:

Verb	Past Tense	Verb	Past Tense
be	*was, were*	*come*	*came*
do	*did*	*say*	*said*
go	*went*	*give*	*gave*

Practice Make an X next to the sentences that use the past-tense verb in the correct way.

1. _____ The sailboat came into port.

2. _____ Junior say that he could not go with us.

3. _____ Megan and Jill tugged at the rope.

4. _____ Shawn give Junior a ticket to the movie.

5. _____ It was a very funny movie.

Verbs (continued)

Find and circle the verb in each sentence. Then write each sentence in the past tense.

6. Jackie goes up to the batter's box.

_____

7. She looks the pitcher in the eye.

_____

8. Swing! She misses the spinning ball.

_____

Apply Read the passages. Draw a line through each verb.
Then write the past-tense form above it.

9. Peter reads his new book as he walks to school.

He bumps into a tree. Peter rubs his head and tries

to smile. He closes his book.

10. Suzy picks flowers in the garden. She

gives them to Mrs. Malcolm. Mrs. Malcolm

puts the flowers in a vase.

Reading and Writing Skills Practice

Name _____ Date _____

Description   *The Dinosaur Who Lived in My Backyard*

Focus Writers give clear descriptions to help readers picture
the story more clearly.

> **Descriptive words** can tell *which* or *how many*.
> Descriptive words can also compare one thing to another.

Identify Look in *The Dinosaur Who Lived in My Backyard*.
Write the sentence that describes the dinosaur egg. Then write
the sentence that describes how big the dinosaur was. Discuss
with your classmates the descriptive words in the sentences.

Page: _____

Sentence that describes the dinosaur egg: _____

_____

_____

Page: _____

Sentence that describes how big the dinosaur was: _____

_____

_____

Description (continued)

Practice and Apply Use your own words to write a sentence
that describes each picture.

1. _____

   _____

2. _____

   _____

3. _____

   _____

Compound Words   Tool Card 67

Focus Using compound words can make your writing more interesting.

> A **compound word** is a word made of two words joined together.
>
>   note + book = notebook
>   grass + hopper = grasshopper
>   snow + flake = snowflake

Practice Circle each compound word.

1.   firefly   sneakers   waterfall

      animal   daylight   baseball

Use the picture clues to make compound words. Write the compound word.

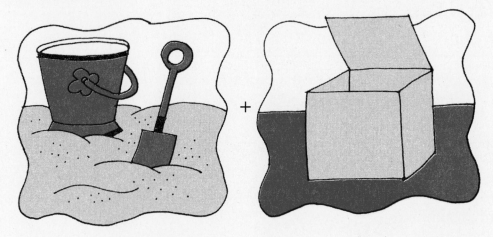

2. _____

Compound Words (continued)

Write a compound word to complete each sentence.
Use the compound words in the box.

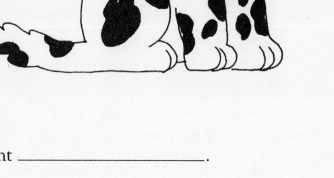

3. The dog carried the _____ to the door.

4. A _____ sat on the leaf.

5. Our coach took us to the

   _____ game.

6. The children grabbed their coats and went _____.

7. Don't forget to wear a _____ in the rain!

8. George found a _____ on the beach.

9. My favorite breakfast is _____.

seashell	ladybug	football
pancakes	raincoat	newspaper
outdoors		

Apply Write a sentence using a compound word from the box
or use a compound word you know.

10. _____

   _____

   _____

   _____

Name _____ Date _____

Time and Order Words   "Why Did the Dinosaurs Disappear?"

Focus The more you know about the time that things happen
in a story and the order in which things happen, the more you
can understand the story.

- Some words tell the **time** or **when** things happen:

    today

    this morning

- Some words tell the **order** in which things happen:

    first

    then

    finally

Identify Look through "Why Did the Dinosaurs Disappear?"
for examples of time and order words. List two examples
of each.

Time Words

_____   _____

Order Words

_____   _____

Time and Order Words
(continued)

Practice and Apply Write a story to go with the pictures. Use words that tell time and order in your story.

_____

_____

_____

_____

_____

_____

_____

_____

Verbs

Focus Past-tense verbs show action that has already happened.

- Many **past-tense verbs** end in -ed.

  walked

- For most one-syllable verbs that have one short vowel and one final consonant, **double the final consonant and add -ed** to form the past tense.

  tapped

- If the verb ends with a consonant followed by y, **change the y to i and add -ed.**

  cried

- Some verbs have special forms:

Verb	Past Tense	Verb	Past Tense
be	was, were	come	came
say	said	meet	met
go	went	eat	ate

Practice Make an X next to each sentence with a verb in the past tense.

1. _____ We went to the store.

2. _____ Mom said we needed some juice.

3. _____ We could buy two oranges.

4. _____ Jess met Carolyn at the children's museum.

5. _____ Together, they will tour the new exhibits.

Verbs (continued)

Find the past-tense form of the verb in each pair of words.
Then write the verb to complete each sentence.

6. see, saw

Michelle _____ three eggs in a nest.

7. watches, watched

For several days, she _____ the eggs.

8. cracked, crack

One day, the eggs _____ open.

9. peeks, peeked

Three tiny heads _____ out.

10. were, are

The baby birds _____ born.

Apply Write a sentence using the past-tense form of
each verb.

11. drip _____

_____

_____

_____

12. cry _____

_____

_____

_____

Reading and Writing Skills Practice

Time and Order Words

The Elves and the Shoemaker

Focus The more you know about the time that things happen and the order in which things happen in a story, the better you can understand the story.

Some words tell the **time** or **when** things happen:

once

tonight

Sometimes writers use phrases to tell the time things happen. A **phrase** is a group of words.

the next morning

Some words tell the **order** in which things happen:

first

next

finally

Identify Look in *The Elves and the Shoemaker* for words and phrases that tell when and in what order things happened. Answer the questions with time and order words or phrases.

When did the shoemaker cut leather? _____

When did he make the shoes? _____

Time and Order Words (continued)

Practice and Apply Read the paragraph and number the pictures to tell the order in which each thing happens.

Sheila made a string of paper trees for her room. First, she folded a piece of paper backward and forward. Next, she drew a tree on the top fold. She made one tree branch run to the folded edge. Then she cut out the tree. She did not cut the branch on the folded edge. Finally, she unfolded the whole paper. She had made a string of trees!

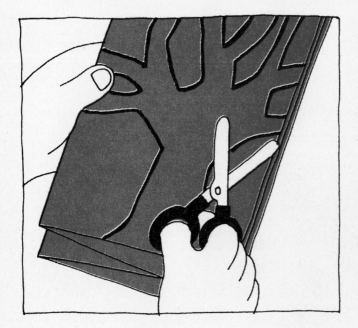

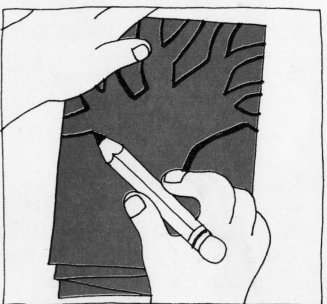

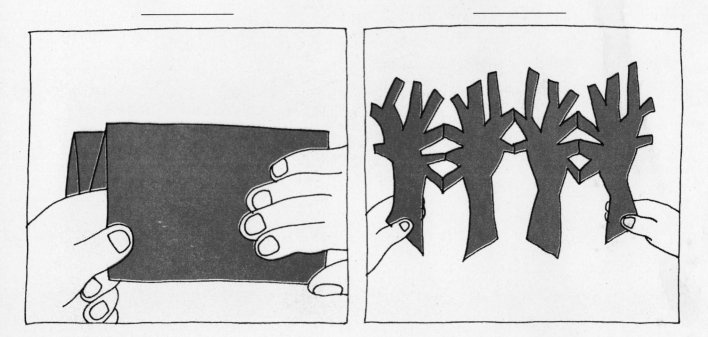

Persuasive Writing

Focus Sometimes writers want to make their readers think, feel, or act a certain way. They want to persuade their readers.

Writers can **persuade** readers by
- giving reasons or facts.
    Puppies make the best pets because they follow you around.
- telling about feelings.
    I always feel happy at the beach.

Practice Make an X next to each sentence that persuades.

1. _____ You should read the story "The Teddy Bears' Picnic" because it will make you smile.

2. _____ The cheetah is the best animal in the world because it is the fastest.

3. _____ Bananas taste better than apples.

4. _____ Eat crunchy oats because they will make you strong.

5. _____ Sheila does not like movies.

Persuasive Writing (continued)

Read the paragraph. Then tell how the writer helps persuade the reader.

Soft clay is much better than clay that gets hard. It is much easier to make something with soft clay. You can make changes if the clay stays soft. After the clay gets hard, you have to start all over!

6. Does the writer give facts or tell feelings?

_____

_____

_____

_____

Apply What is your favorite hobby? Write a paragraph to persuade readers to try your favorite hobby.

7. _____

_____

_____

_____

_____

Reading and Writing Skills Practice

End Punctuation

Focus Every sentence has a punctuation mark at the end. The kind of mark depends on the kind of sentence.

- A sentence that tells something ends with a **period.**
    Kristen is wearing a red shirt.
- A sentence that asks a question ends with a **question mark.**
    Is it a new shirt?
- A sentence that shows strong feeling ends with an **exclamation point.**
    Kristin loves the color red!

Practice Read each sentence and add the correct end punctuation mark. Fill in the circle to show if the sentence tells something, asks a question, or shows strong feeling.

1. I am going to the library_____
   ○ tells   ○ asks   ○ shows strong feeling

2. Wow, that's a great new bike_____
   ○ tells   ○ asks   ○ shows strong feeling

3. Do you have any books I can return for you_____
   ○ tells   ○ asks   ○ shows strong feeling

4. Look at the shooting star_____
   ○ tells   ○ asks   ○ shows strong feeling

5. What kind of soup is this_____
   ○ tells   ○ asks   ○ shows strong feeling

End Punctuation (continued)

Read each sentence and put the correct punctuation mark at the end.

6. Do you know about bicycle safety_____

7. Always wear a helmet_____

8. Stay in the bicycle lanes_____

9. Have you learned the hand signals_____

10. Watch out for that speed bump_____

Apply Write three new sentences using end punctuation marks correctly.

11. Sentence that ends with a period:

_____

_____

_____

12. Sentence that ends with a question mark:

_____

_____

_____

13. Sentence that ends with an exclamation point:

_____

_____

_____

Name _____ Date _____

Giving Reasons

Focus Good writers give reasons for the things that happen in stories.

> Writers **give reasons** to make their ideas clear to readers. Reasons tell why something is the way it is or why characters feel the way they do.

Identify Look through "The Camel's Nose" for an example in which the author gives reasons that answer the question *why?* Write the question and the reasons. Discuss the example with your classmates.

Page: _____

Why? question: _____

_____

_____

Reasons: _____

_____

_____

_____

_____

Giving Reasons (continued)

Practice and Apply Write a one-sentence or two-sentence story to go with each picture. Make sure your story tells what is happening and why.

1. _____

_____

_____

_____

2. _____

_____

_____

_____

Reading and Writing Skills Practice

Name _____ Date _____

Words That Show Place

Focus The more you know about where things happen in a story, the better you can picture what is happening in the story.

> Writers often use clue words that show **place** to let readers know **where** things happen in a story.
>
> *in*
> *on*
> *with*
> *away*

Identify Look through *Corduroy* for clue words that help you picture where events are happening. Write a word that shows place in each sentence. You may use the words in the box for help.

1. Corduroy lived _____ a big store.

2. He waited _____ the shelf with other toys.

3. A little girl wanted to take him home _____ her.

4. Corduroy wandered _____ from the other toys.

on	away	with	in

Reading and Writing Skills Practice

Words That Show Place (continued)

Practice and Apply Look at the picture. Then add your own drawings to the picture. Follow the directions at the bottom of the page.

5. Draw a pillow **on** the bed.

6. Draw a book **on** the bottom shelf of the bookcase.

7. Draw a baseball **beside** the cap.

8. Draw a shoe **under** the bed.

9. Draw a picture **on** the wall.

Reading and Writing Skills Practice

Contractions

Focus Knowing how to make and use contractions can help you be a better writer.

- A **contraction** is one word made of two words put together. One or more letters are left out.
- An **apostrophe (')** takes the place of the missing letters.

  We are going to the lake.

  We're going to the lake. (We + are = We're)

- The words will not are special. To make the contraction, the letters change to make the word **won't.**

Practice Write the two words that make up each contraction.

1. couldn't _____ _____

2. didn't _____ _____

Write the contraction that each pair of words forms.

3. do not _____

4. does not _____

Contractions (continued)

Draw a line to match each pair of words to the correct contraction.

5. he is   he'll

6. he will   I've

7. I have   he's

8. I will   I'll

Rewrite the sentence using a contraction in place of the underlined words.

9. Sea otters <u>are not</u> exactly the same as river otters.

_____

_____

_____

Apply Write two sentences of your own. Use a contraction in each sentence.

10. _____

_____

_____

11. _____

_____

_____

Using Headings

Focus Sometimes writers use headings to separate a long piece of writing into sections to make it easier to read.

> **Headings** are short titles for sections in nonfiction writing. The heading tells what the section is about.

Identify Look in *Clara Barton: Red Cross Pioneer*. Find the heading from the story that matches the information in the outline below.

Page: _____

Heading: _____

In 1869, Clara Barton was tired.

She took a vacation to Europe.

She met Dr. Louis Appia and learned about the Red Cross.

Clara fought for a Red Cross in America.

Finally, the American Red Cross was formed in 1882.

Using Headings (continued)

Practice and Apply Write your own heading for each
paragraph.

Millions of people work for the Red Cross in America.
Most are volunteers. Volunteers work with no pay.
Volunteers know how to help people in emergencies. If
there is a flood or fire, volunteers hand out food. They also
find homes. They give first aid and comfort.

1. Heading: _____

_____

_____

The Red Cross is not only a rescue service. The Red
Cross teaches, too. Many people learn first aid from the Red
Cross. There are Red Cross classes in swimming and
lifesaving. Special classes teach swimming to handicapped
people. Other classes teach safety in the home, outdoors,
and on the water.

2. Heading: _____

_____

_____

Reading and Writing Skills Practice

Writing Paragraphs (Main Idea)   *Clara Barton: Red Cross Pioneer*

Focus A paragraph is a group of sentences that tell about the same idea.

> The most important sentence in a **paragraph** is the **topic sentence** because it tells the main idea, or what all the other sentences are about. Often the topic sentence is the first sentence in a paragraph.

Identify Choose one paragraph from *Clara Barton: Red Cross Pioneer*. Write the topic sentence that tells the main idea of the paragraph. Then write the details the author gives about the idea.

Page: _____

The topic sentence is: _____

_____

_____

Details the author gives about the idea: _____

_____

_____

_____

_____

Writing Paragraphs (continued)

Practice and Apply Use the details that are given at the bottom of the page to write a paragraph about Susan B. Anthony. Be sure to write a topic sentence.

_____

_____

_____

_____

_____

_____

_____

_____

_____

_____

_____

Susan B. Anthony fought for women's rights.
She helped women get the right to vote.
She was a schoolteacher.
She made a newspaper about women's rights.
She voted in an election in 1872 and was arrested.
She died before women got the right to vote.

Reading and Writing Skills Practice

Pronoun/Noun Agreement

Focus Pronouns are words that take the place of nouns. They must agree in number with the nouns they replace. Using the right pronoun makes your meaning clear.

- A **singular (one) pronoun** takes the place of a singular noun.

    Talia drew a picture. Then she colored it.

    Talia drew a picture. Then she colored it.

- **Plural (more than one) pronouns** take the place of plural nouns.

    Jim and Jeremy drew pictures. Then they colored them.

    Jim and Jeremy drew pictures. Then they colored them.

Practice Underline the pronouns and circle the noun or nouns each pronoun replaces.

1. Marla found a kitten in her backyard.

2. The kitten was licking its paw.

3. Marla found a ball. She rolled the ball across the yard.

4. The kitten watched the ball and pounced after it.

Pronoun/Noun Agreement (continued)

Read each numbered sentence. Place an X next to the sentence below it that uses the correct pronoun to replace the underlined word or words.

5. <u>James and his dad</u> went to the beach.

_____ They went to the beach.

_____ He went to the beach.

6. <u>James</u> wanted to swim.

_____ It wanted to swim.

_____ He wanted to swim.

Apply Read the paragraph. Draw a line through each pronoun that does not agree with the noun or nouns it replaces. Write the correct pronoun above the one you crossed out.

Carla and Andrew wanted to clean up the park.

She both took lots of trash bags. Andrew

carried a shovel. They was heavy! The two friends

worked all afternoon in the park. When he were

finished, they was beautiful!

Giving Reasons

Focus Good writers give reasons for the things that happen in stories.

> Writers **give reasons** to make their ideas clear to readers or to give readers answers to things they may wonder about.

Identify Look through *Music, Music for Everyone* for an example in which the author gives reasons that answer the question *why?* Write the question and the reasons.

Page: _____

Why? question: _____

_____

_____

Reasons: _____

_____

_____

_____

_____

Giving Reasons (continued)

Practice and Apply Write a paragraph by adding reasons that
tell why and explain the first sentence in each example.

1. Daniel woke up very early Saturday morning.

_____

_____

_____

_____

_____

2. The students collected all of the trash in the park.

_____

_____

_____

_____

Reading and Writing Skills Practice

Name _____ Date _____

Topic Sentences

Focus A strong topic sentence tells the main idea of the paragraph or what it is all about.

A **topic sentence**
- gives the main idea of the paragraph.
- is often the first sentence of a paragraph. But it is **not always** the first sentence. Sometimes a topic sentence is the last sentence in a paragraph and all the other sentences lead up to it.

Identify Look through *Music, Music for Everyone*. Choose a paragraph with a strong topic sentence. Write the topic sentence, then write the details the author gives about the main idea.

Page: _____

Topic sentence: _____

_____

_____

_____

Details the author gives about the main idea: _____

_____

_____

_____

_____

Topic Sentences (continued)

Practice and Apply Read each paragraph. Underline the topic sentence.

1. <u>Mrs. Stein put Moira in charge of the costumes for our class play.</u> Moira found some long dresses at a thrift shop. She turned them into gowns for the ball. She added feathers, buttons, and shiny ribbons to the long dresses. They were perfect!

2. <u>Brian's dog, Chip, was lost.</u> Brian's friends helped him make signs. The signs said: LOST BLACK AND WHITE DOG NAMED CHIP. PLEASE CALL 555-4584. They nailed the signs on all of the street corners. Brian even put up a sign at the market. Then, he waited by the telephone.

3. Shalene stirred the vegetable soup. It was Grandma's favorite. Shalene added some pepper to the soup. Then she set the table for three—her Dad, herself, and now Grandma, too. <u>Grandma was coming to live with Shalene and her Dad.</u>

Setting

Focus The more you know about the setting of a story, the more you can picture what is happening in the story.

> Writers let readers know about **setting** by giving details that show the **time** and **place** of the action in a story.

Identify Look through *A Pair of Red Clogs* for a sentence that shows how the writer tells readers about the setting. Write the sentence. Then write the words that give details of time and place. Discuss the example with your classmates.

Page: _____

Sentence that shows the setting: _____

_____

_____

_____

_____

What words give details of time and place? _____

_____

_____

_____

Setting (continued)

Practice and Apply Read the passage. Find words and phrases that show time or place to describe the setting. Write the words at the bottom of the page.

    One morning in early fall, Emily and Jane walked down a narrow path that led through the deep woods. The fallen leaves rustled as they plowed through them. Emily liked the way the rising sun gave the purple and gold leaves a warm glow. Jane liked looking up at the long rows of tall trees that lined the path.

Time words that tell about the setting: _____

_____

_____

_____

_____

Place words that tell about the setting: _____

_____

_____

Reading and Writing Skills Practice

Description

Focus Writing good descriptions helps readers form pictures in their minds of people, places, things, or actions.

Good descriptions help readers form pictures by using words that appeal to the senses of *seeing, hearing, smelling, touching,* or *tasting*.

Identify Look through a story you have read for a good description. Write the title of the story and the description. Then tell which of the senses the words in the description appeal to.

Title of story: _____

_____

_____

Description: _____

_____

_____

_____

Which sense does the description appeal to? _____

_____

_____

Description (continued)

Apply Pretend that you are walking through a jungle. Write
some sentences that help your readers form a picture of the
jungle. Use words that describe what you see, hear, smell,
touch, or taste.

_____

_____

_____

_____

_____

_____

_____

_____

_____

_____

_____

_____

Reading and Writing Skills Practice

Name _____ Date _____

Giving Causes

Focus When you read, the more you know about what caused something to happen, the better you will understand what you read.

> Writers **give causes** to explain why an event happened or why a character said or did something. This makes the story clearer to the reader.

Identify Look through "The Boy Who Cried Wolf" for an example of an event. Write the example, then find and write the cause of the event. Discuss the example with your classmates.

Page: _____

Event: _____

_____

_____

_____

Page: _____

Cause: _____

_____

_____

_____

_____

Giving Causes (continued)

Practice and Apply Read the passage, then write answers to the questions.

Ben was late for everything. His friends got angry at him because he was never on time.

One day, some of Ben's friends decided to play a trick on him. They invited him to go to the circus and set up a time and place for all of them to meet. When Ben arrived at the meeting place, his friends were not there. Instead, he found a note telling him to go to Cal's house.

The little boy ran fast. He huffed and puffed all the way. Cal's sister told him the boys had gone to the circus. She said Ben could meet them at the circus gate.

Ben ran to the circus. He stood for hours in front of the circus waiting for his friends. When they did not come, he left.

On his way home, Ben saw his friends playing baseball. He realized that he had been tricked. The little boy was not late for anything again.

1. What happened to Ben? _____

_____

_____

_____

_____

2. What caused this to happen? _____

_____

_____

_____

_____

Reading and Writing Skills Practice

Problems and Solutions

Focus Stories are often exciting because the characters have to solve problems.

- **Problems** are difficult things that happen to characters in a story.

- **Solutions** are ways characters deal with problems.

Identify Look through "Three Hundred Spartans" for an example of a problem. Write the problem and tell how it is solved. Discuss with your classmates how the problem makes the story interesting.

Page: _____

Problem: _____

_____

_____

_____

Page: _____

Solution: _____

_____

_____

_____

Problems and Solutions (continued)

Practice and Apply Read the story, then write the answers to the questions.

Wally was excited because The Great Sardini, the best magician in the world, was coming to town. Wally wanted very much to see The Great Sardini's show. But the show cost five dollars, and Wally only had three dollars saved.

"Sneak in the show for free," his friend Greg told him.

"No," said Wally. "That would be wrong." So Wally went to his father and told him how much he wanted to see The Great Sardini.

"You should earn the money you need," his father said. "If you help me wash the car, I will pay you the money you need."

Wally agreed. He helped to wash the car, and his father paid him the money.

1. What problem did Wally have? _____

_____

_____

2. What was Greg's idea for a solution to Wally's problem? _____

_____

_____

3. Why did Wally say no to Greg's idea? _____

_____

_____

4. How did Wally finally solve his problem? _____

_____

_____

Name _____   Date _____

Giving Information About an Event   "Three Hundred Spartans"

Focus The more information you have about events in stories,
the more likely you are to understand the stories.

> Writers **give details about story events** to make the
> events clearer for the reader.

Identify Look through "Three Hundred Spartans" for an
example of an important story event. Write the example. Then
write the information the author gives to tell about the event.
Discuss the example with your classmates.

Page: _____

Event: _____

_____

_____

_____

Information given: _____

_____

_____

_____

Giving Information About an Event
(continued)

Practice and Apply Read the passage. Then write the event and the details that are given about the event.

At the age of seven, Asher, a Spartan boy, was sent to live in an army barracks. He ate in a common room with other boys his age. They had only a small amount of food. This prepared them for fighting on an empty stomach. A boy caught stealing food was punished by a beating. In winter, the boys slept outdoors without cover.

What happened to Asher? _____

_____

_____

_____

Details given: _____

_____

_____

_____

Giving Examples

Focus Writers give examples to make their ideas clear to readers.

> Writers **give examples** that tell more about an idea. Examples help readers picture the idea so they can understand it better.

Identify Look through *Crow Boy* for an idea that the author makes clear by giving an example for it. Write the idea that is made clear. Then write the example the author gives. Discuss the example with your classmates.

Page: _____

Idea that is made clear: _____

_____

_____

Example the author gives: _____

_____

_____

_____

_____

Giving Examples (continued)

Practice   Draw a line to match the idea with the correct example.

Idea	Example
1. Watching too much TV can get boring.	For instance, there is a new mall on Sixth Street.
2. Our town is growing.	Last night, each time I changed the channel, there was a commercial.
3. We have a good baseball team.	For example, this season we won 10 out of 15 games.

Apply   Look at the ideas and the examples on this page. Write one new example for one of the ideas. Then write the number of the idea.

4. _____

_____

_____

_____

Number: _____

Adjectives and Adverbs

Focus Adjectives are words that describe nouns or pronouns. Adverbs describe verbs.

- **Adjectives** tell how something *looks*, *sounds*, *tastes*, *feels*, or *smells*.
- **Adverbs** usually tell *when*, *where*, or *how*. Many adverbs end in *-ly*.

Practice Read the sentences. Find and write the two adjectives in each sentence.

The spotted dog is in the red barn.

1. _____   _____

My frisky cat is noisy.

2. _____   _____

Write adjectives to complete each sentence.

3. The _____ balloon floats in the _____ sky.

4. The _____ girl leaped into the _____ lake.

5. The _____ clown wore a _____ hat.

6. My _____ sister gave me a _____ book.

Adjectives and Adverbs (continued)

Find and write the adverb in each sentence.

We will eat lunch early this afternoon.

7. _____

Jim ran quickly to catch the bus.

8. _____

Write an adverb that answers the question asked in the second sentence.

       Carlo walks to the front of the room.
       How does Carlo walk to the front of the room?

9. _____

Apply Write a sentence using an adjective and an adverb.
Circle the adjective and underline the adverb.

10. _____

_____

_____

_____

_____

Plot

Focus In stories, the plot tells what happens or happened. Good writers create exciting stories for readers by making each event in a plot lead to another event.

The **plot** of a story
- usually begins by introducing the **main characters,** the **setting,** and the **problem** that must be solved.
- usually ends with a **climax** or high point of the story and a **solution** to the problem.

Identify Look through "The Foolish, Timid Rabbit" for the main characters and write their names. Then find the first important story event. Write about the event in your own words. Discuss the event with your classmates.

Page: _____

Main characters: _____

_____

_____

_____

First important story event: _____

_____

_____

_____

_____

Plot (continued)

Read through "The Foolish, Timid Rabbit." Look for the important events in the story. Then write the answers to the questions.

1. What is the first Rabbit's problem in the story?

_____

_____

_____

2. What did the first Rabbit do?

_____

_____

_____

3. What did the other animals do?

_____

_____

_____

4. How was the problem resolved?

_____

_____

_____

Giving Explanations

Focus Writers give explanations to help readers better understand the ideas presented in stories.

> Writers often **give an explanation** to tell why something is the way it is or to give information about what something means.

Identify Look through "How We Learned the Earth Is Round" for an example of an idea for which the writer gives an explanation. Write the example, then write the explanation of the idea in your own words. Discuss the example with your classmates.

Page: _____

Writer's idea that is being explained: _____

_____

_____

Explanation of the idea: _____

_____

_____

_____

Giving Explanations (continued)

Practice and Apply   Read the passages, then write the answers
to the questions.

The blue whale is the largest animal in the world. An
elephant, a tiger, and a horse could all fit on top of it. The
blue whale can be longer than two train cars.

What is this passage about? _____

_____

What details are given to explain the idea? _____

_____

_____

_____

The spout of water that a whale makes is part of its
breathing process. The blowhole at the top of a whale's head
is a nostril. When the blowhole opens, the whale breathes
in. When the whale breathes out, a mixture of air and water
is forced out of the blowhole.

What is this passage about? _____

_____

What details are given to explain the idea? _____

_____

_____

_____

Descriptive Words

Focus Writers use descriptive words to help readers picture what is being described.

Adjectives are descriptive words. These words are used to describe how something *looks*, *feels*, *smells*, *tastes*, or *sounds* or to tell *how many there are*.

Identify Look through *The Emperor's New Clothes* for examples of words used to describe a story character, an object, or an event. Write an example, then write who or what is being described. Discuss the example with your classmates.

Page: _____

Word used to describe (adjective): _____

_____

What is being described? _____

_____

_____

_____

Descriptive Words (continued)

Practice Read the sentences. Find and write the two descriptive words in each sentence.

1. We like to read funny stories about foolish kings.

   Descriptive word: _____

   Descriptive word: _____

2. The empty piggy bank fell off the slippery table.

   Descriptive word: _____

   Descriptive word: _____

3. The expensive costume was pretty.

   Descriptive word: _____

   Descriptive word: _____

Apply Write a sentence using one descriptive word. Draw a circle around the descriptive word.

4. _____

   _____

   _____

   _____

   _____

Prefixes and Suffixes

Focus Recognizing prefixes and suffixes helps you learn new words and understand their meanings.

- A **prefix** is a syllable added to the beginning of a base word.
- A **suffix** is a syllable added to the end of a base word.

Prefix	Meaning	Example
un-	not	unfair
re-	again	repaint

Suffix	Meaning	Example
-ful	full of	thankful
-less	without	careless
-er	one who does	builder
-ment	act of	enjoyment
-ly	in a way that is	slowly

Practice Circle the word in each sentence that has a prefix or suffix. What does the word mean? Write the meaning on the line.

1. Shirley is unhappy. _____

2. We need to recheck our schedule. _____

3. Mark is always cheerful. _____

4. The farmer is plowing. _____

5. The fearless superhero stopped the train. _____

Prefixes and Suffixes (continued)

Apply Look at the word next to each sentence. Add a prefix or suffix to the word. Write the new word to complete each sentence.

6. quick   The car stopped _____.

7. fear   Charlotte was _____ that her puppy was lost.

8. plant   We need to _____ our garden because rain washed away the seeds.

9. agree   Are we in _____ about our plans?

10. teach   Mr. Walker is the best _____ in the school.

11. even   The boards in the old porch were _____.

12. sing   Marian Anderson was a great _____.

13. hope   It was _____ to try to stop the building from burning.

14. healthy   Spending too much time in the sun is _____.

15. success   The science experiment was _____.

16. quiet   We walked _____ through the library.

17. tell   _____ the story in your own words.

18. entertain   We enjoyed the _____ at the party.

Reading and Writing Skills Practice

Giving Examples

Focus Writers give examples to make their ideas clear to readers.

> Writers **give examples** that tell more about an idea. Examples help readers picture the idea so they can understand it better.

Identify Look through "The First Americans." Find an idea for which the author gives an example that makes the idea clearer. Write the idea that is made clear. Then write the sentence that gives an example or examples to help make the idea clear.

Page: _____

An idea that is made clear: _____

_____

_____

_____

_____

The sentence that gives an example or examples to help make

the idea clear: _____

_____

_____

_____

_____

Giving Examples (continued)

Practice Read the passage. Then write the answers to the questions.

The old gray house was falling down. Floor boards were missing from the front porch. Broken gutters hung from the edge of the worn roof.

1. What is the passage about? _____

_____

2. What details help make the main idea of the passage clear?

_____

_____

_____

Apply Write one sentence that states your idea. Then write two more sentences that give examples to make your idea clear.

3. _____

_____

_____

4. _____

_____

_____

5. _____

_____

_____

Reading and Writing Skills Practice

Name _____ Date _____

Headings and Captions

Focus Writers use headings and captions to organize nonfiction selections.

- **Headings** are short titles for sections in nonfiction writing. The heading tells what the section is about.
- **Captions** are short descriptions that appear with and explain pictures.

Practice Look through a story you have read for one example of a heading. Write the heading and then write what the section is about.

1. Heading: _____

_____

2. What is the section about? _____

_____

_____

Look in a story you have read for one example of a picture with a caption. Write the caption and then write what the caption tells about the picture.

3. Caption: _____

_____

4. What the caption tells about the picture: _____

_____

_____

Reading and Writing Skills Practice

Headings and Captions (continued)

Apply Write a heading for each passage.

People are always interested in weather. Every day they listen to the radio, watch television, and read newspapers to find out what kind of weather they can expect.

5. Heading:

_____

_____

Many famous writers have used "pen names." Pen names are names the writers use that are not their real names. Some writers who used pen names are Mark Twain, whose real name is Samuel Clemens, and Dr. Seuss, whose real name is Theodor Seuss Geisel.

6. Heading:

_____

_____

Write a caption for the picture.

7. Caption:

_____

_____

Reading and Writing Skills Practice

Prefixes and Suffixes

Focus Recognizing prefixes and suffixes in words helps you learn new words and understand their meanings.

- A **prefix** is a syllable added to the beginning of a base word.
- A **suffix** is a syllable added to the end of a base word.

Prefix	Meaning	Example
un-	not	unfair
re-	again	repaint

Suffix	Meaning	Example
-ful	full of	helpful
-less	without	careless

Practice Complete each sentence. Add one of the prefixes or suffixes in the box to the underlined word in the sentence. Write the new word.

1. If you are not <u>afraid</u>, you are _____.

2. If you <u>read</u> a story you have read before, you _____ the story.

3. A doll without <u>hair</u> is _____.

4. A kitten that likes to <u>play</u> is _____.

5. If you <u>fill</u> your cup again, you _____ it.

6. A tool that you cannot <u>use</u> is _____.

Prefixes and Suffixes (continued)

Look at the word next to each sentence. Choose a prefix or a suffix from the box on page 127 and add it to the word. Write the new word to complete the sentence.

7. tied   Sue left her shoelaces _____ so she could take off her shoes easily.

8. fear   Carl was _____ that his cat had shredded his homework.

9. heat   We need to _____ the soup because it doesn't taste good cold.

10. worth   This torn paper is _____.

Apply   Add a suffix or a prefix to each word to make two new words.

11. _____use   **12.** use_____

Now write two sentences using the two new words you made.

13. _____

_____

_____

_____

14. _____

_____

_____

_____

Giving Information About an Event

Focus The more information you have about the events in a story, the more likely you are to understand the story.

> In nonfiction pieces, writers **give information** or **facts** about important events to show that what they say is true or really happened.

Identify Look through "Squanto and the First Thanksgiving" for an example of an important story event. Write the example, then write the information the writer gives to tell about the event. Discuss the example with your classmates.

Page: _____

Event: _____

_____

_____

_____

Important facts about the event: _____

_____

_____

_____

_____

Giving Information
About an Event (continued)

Practice and Apply Read the passage. Then answer the
questions.

In 1622, a ship named the Atocha sank near the coast
of Florida. The Atocha was a Spanish treasure ship packed
with gold, jewels, and silver bars. Hurricane winds and
powerful ocean currents scattered the treasure.

1. What happened to the Atocha? _____

_____

2. When did the event happen? _____

3. Where did the event happen? _____

_____

_____

4. What other important facts are given?

_____

_____

_____

_____

_____

_____

Words That Show Place   "Squanto and the First Thanksgiving"

Focus The more you know about where events happen in a story, the more likely you are to understand and remember the story.

> Writers use **signal words** to let readers know where parts of a story take place.
>
> | Signal Word | Example |
> |---|---|
> | in | in Spain |
> | by | by the ocean |
> | from | from Africa |

Identify Look through "Squanto and the First Thanksgiving" for an example of how the writer uses signal words to show place. Write the sentence, then write the signal word or words from the sentence. Discuss the example with your classmates.

Page: _____

Sentence with signal word in it: _____

_____

_____

Word or words that show place: _____

_____

Words That Show Place (continued)

Practice Look at the picture, then read the sentences. Complete each sentence by writing the signal word that correctly shows the place of the bird and the man in the picture.

1. The bird landed _____ Joe's head.

2. Joe stood _____ the fancy birdcage.

Apply Look at the picture, then write two sentences about the picture. Use signal words to tell where things are in the picture.

3. _____

_____

4. _____

_____

Reading and Writing Skills Practice

Name _____ Date _____

Giving Causes   "James Forten, Hero and True Friend"

Focus Writers give causes to made their ideas clearer.

> Writers **give causes** to explain why an event happened or
> why a character feels a certain way.

Identify Look through "James Forten, Hero and True Friend."
Find an example of how the writer gives causes to tell why a
character feels a certain way. Write how the character feels,
then write what caused the character to feel this way. Discuss
the example with your classmates.

Page: _____

How does the character feel? _____

_____

_____

_____

_____

What caused the character to feel this way? _____

_____

_____

_____

_____

Giving Causes (continued)

Practice and Apply Read the passage. Then write the answers to the questions.

Fred was feeling lonely because his friends were away at camp. Then Fred remembered his cousin Arnold who lived in another city. Fred wrote a letter to Arnold. He asked Arnold to come and visit for the summer.

Arnold said yes! Now, even though Fred's friends are gone, he doesn't feel lonely anymore because he knows he will soon have his cousin to play with.

1. How did Fred feel? _____

_____

_____

2. What caused Fred to feel this way? _____

_____

_____

3. What did Fred do? _____

_____

_____

4. What caused Fred to feel better?

_____

_____

_____

Reading and Writing Skills Practice

Adjectives and Adverbs

Focus Adjectives describe nouns or pronouns. Adverbs describe verbs.

- **Adjectives** tell about a person, a place, or a thing.
  I bought a **red** coat.
- **Adverbs** usually tell *when*, *where*, or *how*. Many adverbs end in *-ly*.
  She ran **fast.**

Practice Read the sentences. Write the adjectives that describe the noun in each sentence.

1. Today is a gloomy day.   _____

2. The day is cloudy and cold.   _____

3. Sally wears a big, furry hat.   _____

4. We laughed at the funny story.   _____

Write the adverb that describes the action in each sentence.

5. We walk quickly down the street.   _____

6. We don't want to be late.   _____

7. I will return soon.   _____

8. The dog chewed slowly.   _____

Adjectives and Adverbs (continued)

Find and underline the adverb in each sentence.

9. Our family eats breakfast early in the morning. (When)

10. The children boarded the bus quickly. (How)

11. The ducks swam away from shore. (Where)

Write an adverb to complete the sentences.

12. The deer ran _____.

13. The lions roared _____.

Read the sentences. Then write adjectives to describe how the nouns in the sentences look, taste, feel, or smell.

14. Our grocery cart was filled with _____ peppers and

_____ beans.

15. The garden has _____ flowers.

Apply Write one sentence about something that happened at school. Use one adjective and one adverb. Circle the adjective and underline the adverb.

16. _____

_____

_____

_____

Name _____ Date _____

Commas in Dates, Addresses, and Parts of a Letter

Tool Card 49

Focus Using commas correctly makes writing clearer.

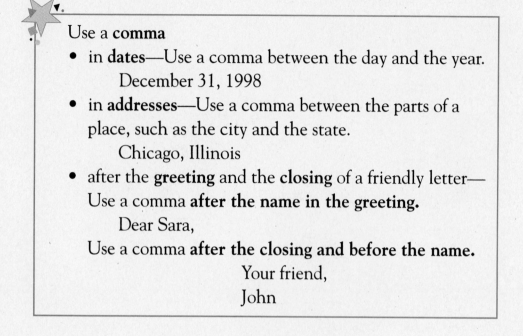

Use a **comma**
- in **dates**—Use a comma between the day and the year.
    December 31, 1998
- in **addresses**—Use a comma between the parts of a place, such as the city and the state.
    Chicago, Illinois
- after the **greeting** and the **closing** of a friendly letter—
Use a comma **after the name in the greeting.**
    Dear Sara,
Use a comma **after the closing and before the name.**
        Your friend,
        John

Practice Place commas where they are needed.

1. San Francisco California

2. July 4 1996

3. Dear Sally

4. Your friend Jane

5. I went to Houston Texas.

6. Today is October 28 1998.

Commas in Dates, Addresses, and Parts of a Letter
(continued)

Read the letter. Put commas where they are needed.

May 16, 1997

Dear Jenny,

Could you please come to our class party at 2 o'clock on June 16, 1997? We are going to celebrate winning the state spelling bee. It was held in Boston, Massachusetts.

Please let us know by June 1 if you are coming.

Mrs. Brown

Apply Write your birth date. Then write the birth date of a friend. Put commas in the correct places.

Your birth date: _____

Your friend's birth date: _____

Name _____ Date _____

Giving Definitions

Focus In stories, the more you know about what the words mean, the more likely you are to understand and enjoy the stories.

- A **definition** gives the meaning of a word.
- In stories, writers **give definitions** of words or phrases that may be hard for readers to understand.

Identify Look through "La Florida" for examples in which the writer gives a definition of a word or a phrase. Write one example. Discuss the example with your classmates.

Page: _____

Word or phrase that is defined: _____

_____

_____

Definition that is given: _____

_____

_____

_____

Giving Definitions (continued)

Practice Read the passage and answer the questions. Then write a sentence using the word for which the writer gives a definition.

Explorers are people who travel to places about which we know very little. They learn about the natural features of the place and about the people who live there.

1. What word is defined? _____

_____

2. What is the meaning of the word? _____

_____

_____

3. Write a sentence using the defined word:

_____

_____

_____

Apply Write a sentence giving the definition of a word whose meaning you know to help make the meaning clear for readers.

4. _____

_____

_____

Name _____ Date _____

Description

Focus Writers use details in their descriptions to help readers picture the scene.

- A **description** might tell how something or someone *looks*, *feels*, *smells*, *tastes*, or *sounds*.

- Writers use descriptions that appeal to the senses to make a story more interesting for readers.

Identify Look through "East Meets West" for examples of good descriptions. Write one sentence that contains a description. Then write what is being described. Discuss the example with your classmates.

Page: _____

Sentence with description: _____

_____

_____

_____

_____

What is the author describing? _____

_____

Description (continued)

Practice Read the passage. Write all the words that describe the train, then answer the question.

      The long black train puffed, thundered, and clanged down the track. From a distance, we could see its engine's bright white headlight.

1. Words that describe the train: _____

_____

_____

_____

2. Which of the senses does the description appeal to?

_____

_____

Apply Write a sentence giving a description of something in your classroom. Use words that describe how it looks, feels, smells, sounds, or tastes.

3. _____

_____

_____

_____

_____

Commas in Dates, Addresses, and Parts of a Letter

Tool Card 49

Focus Using commas correctly makes writing clearer.

Use a **comma**
- in **dates**—Use a comma between the day and the year.
    January 6, 1997
- in **addresses**—Use a comma between the parts of a place.
    Rome, Italy
- after the **greeting** and the **closing** of a friendly letter
  Use a comma **after the name in the greeting.**
        Dear Kent,
  Use a comma **after the closing and before the name.**
        Your friend,
        Jean

Practice Place commas where they are needed in each sentence.

1. Katie danced in her first recital on May 8 1996.

2. Jim started kindergarten at the Truman School in Detroit Michigan.

3. Sandra signed her letter to Susan like this:

Your pal

Sandra

Commas in Dates, Addresses, and Parts of a Letter (continued)

Look at the envelope. Put commas where they are needed in the return address and in the address.

4.

Miss Julia Green
243 Market Street
Chicago IL 60656

Mr. Edmund Grant
42 Rue d'Orlaine
Paris France

Read the letter. Put commas where they are needed.

5.

June 14 1997

Dear Ed

The week of August 6 is a good time for me to visit you. I am so excited about seeing you in Paris France. Please tell me what to pack.

Your friend

Julia

Apply Write your own address. Put commas where they are needed.

6. _____

_____

_____